Book Title

Author _____ Nationality _____

Genre _____ Year _____ Pages _____

Memorable Quote	Page Number

Characters

Plot Summary

Notes

Rating ☆ ☆ ☆ ☆ ☆

Book Title

Author

Nationality

Genre

Year

Pages

Memorable Quote	Page Number

Characters

Plot Summary

Notes

Rating ☆ ☆ ☆ ☆ ☆

Book Title

Author _____   Nationality _____

Genre _____   Year _____   Pages ____

Memorable Quote	Page Number

Characters

Plot Summary

Notes

Rating ☆ ☆ ☆ ☆ ☆

Book Title

Author

Nationality

Genre

Year

Pages

Memorable Quote	Page Number

Characters

Plot Summary

Notes

Rating ☆ ☆ ☆ ☆ ☆

Book Title

Author   Nationality

Genre   Year   Pages

Memorable Quote	Page Number

Characters

Plot Summary

Notes

Rating ☆ ☆ ☆ ☆ ☆

Book Title

Author _____ Nationality _____

Genre _____ Year _____ Pages _____

Memorable Quote	Page Number

Characters

Plot Summary

Notes

Rating ☆ ☆ ☆ ☆ ☆

Book Title

Author _____   Nationality _____

Genre _____   Year _____   Pages _____

Memorable Quote	Page Number

Characters

Plot Summary

Notes

Rating   ☆ ☆ ☆ ☆ ☆

Book Title

Author

Nationality

Genre

Year

Pages

Memorable Quote	Page Number

Characters

Plot Summary

Notes

Rating ☆ ☆ ☆ ☆ ☆

Book Title

Author: _____ Nationality: _____

Genre: _____ Year: _____ Pages: _____

Memorable Quote	Page Number

Characters

Plot Summary

Notes

Rating ☆ ☆ ☆ ☆ ☆

Book Title

Author: _____ Nationality: _____

Genre: _____ Year: _____ Pages: _____

Memorable Quote	Page Number

Characters

Plot Summary

Notes

Rating ☆ ☆ ☆ ☆ ☆

Book Title

Author: _____ Nationality: _____

Genre: _____ Year: _____ Pages: _____

Memorable Quote	Page Number

Characters

Plot Summary

Notes

Rating ☆ ☆ ☆ ☆ ☆

Book Title

Author: _____   Nationality: _____

Genre: _____   Year: _____   Pages: _____

Memorable Quote	Page Number

Characters

Plot Summary

Notes

Rating ☆ ☆ ☆ ☆ ☆

Book Title

Author   Nationality

Genre   Year   Pages

Memorable Quote	Page Number

Characters

Plot Summary

Notes

Rating ☆ ☆ ☆ ☆ ☆

Book Title

Author _____ Nationality _____

Genre _____ Year _____ Pages _____

Memorable Quote	Page Number

Characters

Plot Summary

Notes

Rating ☆ ☆ ☆ ☆ ☆

Book Title

Author: _____   Nationality: _____

Genre: _____   Year: _____   Pages: _____

Memorable Quote	Page Number

Characters

Plot Summary

Notes

Rating ☆ ☆ ☆ ☆ ☆

Book Title

Author _____ Nationality _____

Genre _____ Year _____ Pages _____

Memorable Quote	Page Number

Characters

Plot Summary

Notes

Rating ☆ ☆ ☆ ☆ ☆

Book Title

Author _____ Nationality _____

Genre _____ Year _____ Pages _____

Memorable Quote	Page Number

Characters

Plot Summary

Notes

Rating ☆ ☆ ☆ ☆ ☆

Book Title

Author _____ **Nationality** _____

Genre _____ **Year** _____ **Pages** _____

Memorable Quote	Page Number

Characters

Plot Summary

Notes

Rating ☆ ☆ ☆ ☆ ☆

Book Title

Author: _____ Nationality: _____

Genre: _____ Year: _____ Pages: _____

Memorable Quote	Page Number

Characters

Plot Summary

Notes

Rating ☆ ☆ ☆ ☆ ☆

Book Title

Author: _____ Nationality: _____

Genre: _____ Year: _____ Pages: _____

Memorable Quote	Page Number

Characters

Plot Summary

Notes

Rating ☆ ☆ ☆ ☆ ☆

Book Title

Author: _____   Nationality: _____

Genre: _____   Year: _____   Pages: _____

Memorable Quote	Page Number

Characters

Plot Summary

Notes

Rating ☆ ☆ ☆ ☆ ☆

Book Title

Author: _____ Nationality: _____

Genre: _____ Year: _____ Pages: _____

Memorable Quote	Page Number

Characters

Plot Summary

Notes

Rating ☆ ☆ ☆ ☆ ☆

Book Title

Author _____   Nationality _____

Genre _____   Year _____   Pages _____

Memorable Quote	Page Number

Characters

Plot Summary

Notes

Rating ☆ ☆ ☆ ☆ ☆

Book Title

Author   Nationality

Genre   Year   Pages

Memorable Quote	Page Number

Characters

Plot Summary

Notes

Rating ☆ ☆ ☆ ☆ ☆

Book Title

Author

Nationality

Genre

Year

Pages

Memorable Quote	Page Number

Characters

Plot Summary

Notes

Rating ☆ ☆ ☆ ☆ ☆

Book Title

Author

Nationality

Genre

Year

Pages

Memorable Quote	Page Number

Characters

Plot Summary

Notes

Rating ☆ ☆ ☆ ☆ ☆

Book Title

Author: _____   Nationality: _____

Genre: _____   Year: _____   Pages: _____

Memorable Quote	Page Number

Characters

Plot Summary

Notes

Rating ☆ ☆ ☆ ☆ ☆

Book Title

Author _____ Nationality _____

Genre _____ Year _____ Pages _____

Memorable Quote	Page Number

Characters

Plot Summary

Notes

Rating ☆ ☆ ☆ ☆ ☆

Book Title

Author

Nationality

Genre

Year

Pages

Memorable Quote	Page Number

Characters

Plot Summary

Notes

Rating ☆ ☆ ☆ ☆ ☆

Book Title

Author   Nationality

Genre   Year   Pages

Memorable Quote	Page Number

Characters

Plot Summary

Notes

Rating ☆ ☆ ☆ ☆ ☆

Book Title

Author _____ Nationality _____

Genre _____ Year _____ Pages _____

Memorable Quote	Page Number

Characters

Plot Summary

Notes

Rating ☆ ☆ ☆ ☆ ☆

Book Title

Author　　　　　　　　Nationality

Genre　　　　　　　　　Year　　　　　　　　Pages

Memorable Quote	Page Number

Characters

Plot Summary

Notes

Rating ☆ ☆ ☆ ☆ ☆

Book Title

Author _____   Nationality _____

Genre _____   Year _____   Pages _____

Memorable Quote	Page Number

Characters

Plot Summary

Notes

Rating ☆ ☆ ☆ ☆ ☆

Book Title

Author _____ Nationality _____

Genre _____ Year _____ Pages _____

Memorable Quote	Page Number

Characters

Plot Summary

Notes

Rating ☆ ☆ ☆ ☆ ☆

Book Title

Author _____   Nationality _____

Genre _____   Year _____   Pages _____

Memorable Quote	Page Number

Characters

Plot Summary

Notes

Rating ☆ ☆ ☆ ☆ ☆

Book Title

Author

Nationality

Genre

Year

Pages

Memorable Quote	Page Number

Characters

Plot Summary

Notes

Rating ☆ ☆ ☆ ☆ ☆

Book Title

Author
Genre
Nationality
Year
Pages

Memorable Quote	Page Number

Characters

Plot Summary

Notes

Rating ☆ ☆ ☆ ☆ ☆

Book Title

Author _____   Nationality _____

Genre _____   Year _____   Pages ____

Memorable Quote	Page Number

Characters

Plot Summary

Notes

Rating ☆ ☆ ☆ ☆ ☆

Book Title

Author   Nationality

Genre   Year   Pages

Memorable Quote	Page Number

Characters

Plot Summary

Notes

Rating   ☆ ☆ ☆ ☆ ☆

Book Title

Author

Nationality

Genre

Year

Pages

Memorable Quote	Page Number

Characters

Plot Summary

Notes

Rating ☆ ☆ ☆ ☆ ☆

Book Title

Author _____ Nationality _____

Genre _____ Year _____ Pages _____

Memorable Quote	Page Number

Characters

Plot Summary

Notes

Rating ☆ ☆ ☆ ☆ ☆

Book Title

Author _____ Nationality _____

Genre _____ Year _____ Pages _____

Memorable Quote	Page Number

Characters

Plot Summary

Notes

Rating ☆ ☆ ☆ ☆ ☆

Book Title

Author _____   Nationality _____

Genre _____   Year _____   Pages _____

Memorable Quote	Page Number

Characters

Plot Summary

Notes

Rating ☆ ☆ ☆ ☆ ☆

Book Title

Author Nationality

Genre Year Pages

Memorable Quote	Page Number

Characters

Plot Summary

Notes

Rating ☆ ☆ ☆ ☆ ☆

Book Title

Author _____ Nationality _____

Genre _____ Year _____ Pages _____

Memorable Quote	Page Number

Characters

Plot Summary

Notes

Rating ☆ ☆ ☆ ☆ ☆

Book Title

Author _____   Nationality _____

Genre _____   Year _____   Pages _____

Memorable Quote	Page Number

Characters

Plot Summary

Notes

Rating ☆ ☆ ☆ ☆ ☆

Book Title

Author _____   Nationality _____

Genre _____   Year _____   Pages _____

Memorable Quote	Page Number

Characters

Plot Summary

Notes

Rating ☆ ☆ ☆ ☆ ☆

Book Title _____

Author _____   Nationality _____

Genre _____   Year _____   Pages _____

Memorable Quote	Page Number

Characters

Plot Summary

Notes

Rating ☆ ☆ ☆ ☆ ☆

Book Title

Author: _____ Nationality: _____

Genre: _____ Year: _____ Pages: _____

Memorable Quote	Page Number

Characters

Plot Summary

Notes

Rating ☆ ☆ ☆ ☆ ☆

Book Title

Author: _____ Nationality: _____

Genre: _____ Year: _____ Pages: _____

Memorable Quote	Page Number

Characters

Plot Summary

Notes

Rating ☆ ☆ ☆ ☆ ☆

Book Title

Author _____ Nationality _____

Genre _____ Year _____ Pages _____

Memorable Quote	Page Number

Characters

Plot Summary

Notes

Rating ☆ ☆ ☆ ☆ ☆

Book Title

Author: _____   Nationality: _____

Genre: _____   Year: _____   Pages: _____

Memorable Quote	Page Number

Characters

Plot Summary

Notes

Rating ☆ ☆ ☆ ☆ ☆

Book Title

Author

Nationality

Genre

Year

Pages

Memorable Quote	Page Number

Characters

Plot Summary

Notes

Rating ☆ ☆ ☆ ☆ ☆

Book Title

Author

Nationality

Genre

Year

Pages

Memorable Quote	Page Number

Characters

Plot Summary

Notes

Rating ☆ ☆ ☆ ☆ ☆

Book Title

Author _____ Nationality _____

Genre _____ Year _____ Pages _____

Memorable Quote	Page Number

Characters

Plot Summary

Notes

Rating ☆ ☆ ☆ ☆ ☆

Book Title

Author _____ Nationality _____

Genre _____ Year _____ Pages _____

Memorable Quote	Page Number

Characters

Plot Summary

Notes

Rating ☆ ☆ ☆ ☆ ☆

Book Title

Author: _____ Nationality: _____

Genre: _____ Year: _____ Pages: _____

Memorable Quote	Page Number

Characters

Plot Summary

Notes

Rating ☆ ☆ ☆ ☆ ☆

Book Title

Author _____   Nationality _____

Genre _____   Year _____   Pages _____

Memorable Quote	Page Number

Characters

Plot Summary

Notes

Rating ☆ ☆ ☆ ☆ ☆

Book Title

Author   Nationality

Genre   Year   Pages

Memorable Quote	Page Number

Characters

Plot Summary

Notes

Rating ☆ ☆ ☆ ☆ ☆

Book Title

Author _____   Nationality _____

Genre _____   Year _____   Pages _____

Memorable Quote	Page Number

Characters

Plot Summary

Notes

Rating ☆ ☆ ☆ ☆ ☆

Book Title

Author _____   Nationality _____

Genre _____   Year _____   Pages _____

Memorable Quote	Page Number

Characters

Plot Summary

Notes

Rating ☆ ☆ ☆ ☆ ☆

Book Title

Author _____   Nationality _____

Genre _____   Year _____   Pages _____

Memorable Quote	Page Number

Characters

Plot Summary

Notes

Rating ☆ ☆ ☆ ☆ ☆

Book Title

Author: _____   Nationality: _____

Genre: _____   Year: _____   Pages: _____

Memorable Quote	Page Number

Characters

Plot Summary

Notes

Rating ☆ ☆ ☆ ☆ ☆

Book Title

Author   Nationality

Genre   Year   Pages

Memorable Quote	Page Number

Characters

Plot Summary

Notes

Rating ☆ ☆ ☆ ☆ ☆

Book Title

Author _____   Nationality _____

Genre _____   Year _____   Pages _____

Memorable Quote	Page Number

Characters

Plot Summary

Notes

Rating ☆ ☆ ☆ ☆ ☆

Book Title

Author: _____ Nationality: _____

Genre: _____ Year: _____ Pages: _____

Memorable Quote	Page Number

Characters

Plot Summary

Notes

Rating ☆ ☆ ☆ ☆ ☆

Book Title

Author: _____ Nationality: _____

Genre: _____ Year: _____ Pages: _____

Memorable Quote	Page Number

Characters

Plot Summary

Notes

Rating ☆ ☆ ☆ ☆ ☆

Book Title

Author _____ Nationality _____

Genre _____ Year _____ Pages _____

Memorable Quote	Page Number

Characters

Plot Summary

Notes

Rating ☆ ☆ ☆ ☆ ☆

Book Title

Author: _____   Nationality: _____

Genre: _____   Year: _____   Pages: _____

Memorable Quote	Page Number

Characters

Plot Summary

Notes

Rating ☆ ☆ ☆ ☆ ☆

Book Title

Author

Nationality

Genre

Year

Pages

Memorable Quote	Page Number

Characters

Plot Summary

Notes

Rating ☆ ☆ ☆ ☆ ☆

Book Title

Author: _____   Nationality: _____

Genre: _____   Year: _____   Pages: _____

Memorable Quote	Page Number

Characters

Plot Summary

Notes

Rating ☆ ☆ ☆ ☆ ☆

Book Title

Author: _____ Nationality: _____

Genre: _____ Year: _____ Pages: _____

Memorable Quote	Page Number

Characters

Plot Summary

Notes

Rating ☆ ☆ ☆ ☆ ☆

Book Title

Author _____   Nationality _____

Genre _____   Year _____   Pages _____

Memorable Quote	Page Number

Characters

Plot Summary

Notes

Rating ☆ ☆ ☆ ☆ ☆

Book Title

Author: _____   Nationality: _____

Genre: _____   Year: _____   Pages: _____

Memorable Quote	Page Number

Characters

Plot Summary

Notes

Rating ☆ ☆ ☆ ☆ ☆

Book Title

Author _____ Nationality _____

Genre _____ Year _____ Pages _____

Memorable Quote	Page Number

Characters

Plot Summary

Notes

Rating ☆ ☆ ☆ ☆ ☆

Book Title _____

Author _____   Nationality _____

Genre _____   Year _____   Pages _____

Memorable Quote	Page Number

Characters

Plot Summary

Notes

Rating ☆ ☆ ☆ ☆ ☆

Book Title

Author _____ Nationality _____

Genre _____ Year _____ Pages _____

Memorable Quote	Page Number

Characters

Plot Summary

Notes

Rating ☆ ☆ ☆ ☆ ☆

Book Title

Author

Nationality

Genre

Year

Pages

Memorable Quote	Page Number

Characters

Plot Summary

Notes

Rating ☆ ☆ ☆ ☆ ☆

Book Title

Author: _____   Nationality: _____

Genre: _____   Year: _____   Pages: _____

Memorable Quote	Page Number

Characters

Plot Summary

Notes

Rating ☆ ☆ ☆ ☆ ☆

Book Title

Author

Nationality

Genre

Year

Pages

Memorable Quote	Page Number

Characters

Plot Summary

Notes

Rating ☆ ☆ ☆ ☆ ☆

Book Title

Author　　　　　　　　　　Nationality

Genre　　　　　　　　　　Year　　　　　　　　Pages

Memorable Quote	Page Number

Characters

Plot Summary

Notes

Rating ☆ ☆ ☆ ☆ ☆

Book Title

Author: _____ Nationality: _____

Genre: _____ Year: _____ Pages: _____

Memorable Quote	Page Number

Characters

Plot Summary

Notes

Rating ☆ ☆ ☆ ☆ ☆

Book Title

Author   Nationality

Genre   Year   Pages

Memorable Quote	Page Number

Characters

Plot Summary

Notes

Rating ☆ ☆ ☆ ☆ ☆

Book Title

Author
Nationality
Genre
Year
Pages

Memorable Quote	Page Number

Characters

Plot Summary

Notes

Rating ☆ ☆ ☆ ☆ ☆

Book Title

Author _____   Nationality _____

Genre _____   Year _____   Pages _____

Memorable Quote	Page Number

Characters

Plot Summary

Notes

Rating ☆ ☆ ☆ ☆ ☆

Book Title

Author: _____ **Nationality:** _____

Genre: _____ **Year:** _____ **Pages:** _____

Memorable Quote	Page Number

Characters

Plot Summary

Notes

Rating ☆ ☆ ☆ ☆ ☆

Book Title

Author _____ Nationality _____

Genre _____ Year _____ Pages _____

Memorable Quote	Page Number

Characters

Plot Summary

Notes

Rating ☆ ☆ ☆ ☆ ☆

Book Title

Author _____   Nationality _____

Genre _____   Year _____   Pages ___

Memorable Quote	Page Number

Characters

Plot Summary

Notes

Rating ☆ ☆ ☆ ☆ ☆

Book Title

Author _____ Nationality _____

Genre _____ Year _____ Pages _____

Memorable Quote	Page Number

Characters

Plot Summary

Notes

Rating ☆ ☆ ☆ ☆ ☆

Book Title

Author _____ Nationality _____

Genre _____ Year _____ Pages _____

Memorable Quote	Page Number

Characters

Plot Summary

Notes

Rating ☆ ☆ ☆ ☆ ☆

Book Title

Author: _____   Nationality: _____

Genre: _____   Year: _____   Pages: _____

Memorable Quote	Page Number

Characters

Plot Summary

Notes

Rating ☆ ☆ ☆ ☆ ☆

Book Title

Author _____ Nationality _____

Genre _____ Year _____ Pages _____

Memorable Quote	Page Number

Characters

Plot Summary

Notes

Rating ☆ ☆ ☆ ☆ ☆

Book Title

Author _____ Nationality _____

Genre _____ Year _____ Pages _____

Memorable Quote	Page Number

Characters

Plot Summary

Notes

Rating ☆ ☆ ☆ ☆ ☆

Book Title

Author

Nationality

Genre

Year

Pages

Memorable Quote	Page Number

Characters

Plot Summary

Notes

Rating ☆ ☆ ☆ ☆ ☆

Book Title

Author   Nationality

Genre   Year   Pages

Memorable Quote	Page Number

Characters

Plot Summary

Notes

Rating ☆ ☆ ☆ ☆ ☆

Book Title

Author: _____ Nationality: _____

Genre: _____ Year: _____ Pages: _____

Memorable Quote	Page Number

Characters

Plot Summary

Notes

Rating ☆ ☆ ☆ ☆ ☆

Book Title

Author _____   Nationality _____

Genre _____   Year _____   Pages _____

Memorable Quote	Page Number

Characters

Plot Summary

Notes

Rating ☆ ☆ ☆ ☆ ☆

Book Title

Author _____ Nationality _____

Genre _____ Year _____ Pages _____

Memorable Quote	Page Number

Characters

Plot Summary

Notes

Rating ☆ ☆ ☆ ☆ ☆

Book Title

Author   Nationality

Genre   Year   Pages

Memorable Quote	Page Number

Characters

Plot Summary

Notes

Rating ☆ ☆ ☆ ☆ ☆

Book Title

Author

Nationality

Genre

Year

Pages

Memorable Quote	Page Number

Characters

Plot Summary

Notes

Rating ☆ ☆ ☆ ☆ ☆